Grits™

Girls Raised In The South

Southern Appeal, Inc.   129 Citation Court   Suite 111
Birmingham, Alabama 35209
1-888-45GRITS

Girls Raised In The South

ISBN 1-891005-00-6

Printed in the United States

Dedication

To Sarah Ford Ricketson,

a true Southern lady,

who wrote to her son,

Jim Ford, Jr.,

"There <u>is</u>

something

special

about the South."

Grits™
Girls Raised In The South

by

Deborah Ford & Paula Bennett

Illustrated by Nana Patricia

GRITS

Girls Raised In The South

What makes Southern women extraordinary?
It's everything from our manners (impeccable) to
our expectations (always high) and
our style (classy).
We're remarkably distinct and hopelessly in love with our history and
tradition. Known the world over for our femininity, charm, hospitality,
and beauty, we're Girls Raised In The South, and we're mighty proud
of all this says to the world.
After all, those below the Mason-Dixon line know
a perfect world -- -- RC Cola, Moon Pies, and a Southern girl.
So from our unique perspective,
here's what Southern women know about living in Dixie,
the best part of these great United States.

Southern girls know their memorable couples

Priscilla and Elvis
Zelda and Scott
Scarlett and Rhett

Southern girls know the three
types of school
Ballroom
Ballet
Charm

Southern girls know the three M's
Moonlight
Magnolias   Mint Juleps

Southern girls don't drink, they sip ...a lot

Southern girls appreciate their natural assets
Dewy skin
A winning smile
That unforgettable Southern drawl

Southern girls have a distinct way
with fond expressions
"Y'all come back!"
"Well, bless your heart."
"Drop by when you can."
"How's your mother?"
"Love your hair."

Southern girls know their manners
Yes, m'am   Yes, sir
Why, no, Billy!

Southern girls know their summer
weather report
Humidity
Humidity
Humidity

Southern girls have
more fun than
should be allowed

Southern girls know their men with silver tongues

Jimmy Swaggert   Jim Bakker

Ernest Angley

Southern girls know their great musicians

Elvis

Elvis

Elvis

Southern girls know how to loosen a tongue with a
Southern touch

Wild Turkey   Jack Daniels   Jim Beam

Southern girls know their three R's

Rich

Richer

Richest

Southern girls know their gentlemen with soul

Percy Sledge

B.B.King

Ray Charles

Otis Redding

James Brown

Southern girls know the joys of June, July, and
August
Summer tans
Wide brimmed hats
Strapless sun dresses

Southern girls are always
in high cotton

Southern girls know everybody's first name
Honey
Darlin'
Sugah

Southern girls know the movies that speak to their hearts
Gone With the Wind
Fried Green Tomatoes at the Whistle Stop Cafe
Driving Miss Daisy
Steel Magnolias

Southern girls know their women with
unleashed ambition
Tammy Faye Bakker   Marla Trump
Hillary Clinton

Southern girls know where to go to have a good time
Sugartit, Kentucky
Smut Eye, Alabama
Romance, Arkansas
Dewey Rose, Georgia
Bourbon, Mississippi
Welcome, North Carolina

Southern girls know the easy directions
to the South
Drive below the Mason-Dixon line and look for
Kentucky bluegrass
Alabama kudzu
Spanish moss hanging
from live oak trees

Southern girls love
to sin
and tell about it!

Southern girls know how to eat watermelon on a hot summer day

Plenty of napkins, Salt, and dahlin', Leave your good clothes at home

Southern girls know the variations on the great subject of down-home BBQ

Inside/Outside

Chopped   Pulled

Sliced

Soppin' with vinegar, tomato, or mustard sauce

Southern girls know their GRITS

Cheese   Stoneground

Garlic   Instant

Southern girls know their greens
Kale
Poke Sallet
Mustard
Collards
Dandelions
Turnips
...all served with hot vinegar sauce

Southern girls have
vine ripe
tomatoes

Southern girls know their religions
Baptist
Methodist
Football

Southern girls know the four seasons
Recruiting
Spring Training
Practice
Football

Southern girls
know
their
primary
colors

Southern girls know their brothers and sisters
who can turn a big profit
Sam Walton   Colonel Sanders
Mary Kay   Ted Turner

Southern girls know their women of great letters
Margaret Mitchell   Eudora Welty
Harper Lee
And how could we forget Vanna White?

Southern girls know their sisters that
entertain the world
Dixie Carter
Dolly Parton
Tina Turner
Oprah Winfrey
and
Fannie Flagg

Southern girls know their just desserts
Banana puddin'
Pineapple upside down cake
Homemade ice cream
Peach cobbler
Pecan and sweet potato pie

Southern girls know their country breakfasts
Red-eye gravy
GRITS
Country ham
Mouth watering homemade biscuits